OSCAR WILDE

Quotations

JARROLD
PUBLISHING

$\mathcal{M}$ost people are other people.
Their thoughts are someone
else's opinion, their life a mimicry,
their passions a quotation.

De Profundis

The world is a stage, but the play is badly cast.

Lord Arthur Savile's Crime

$\mathbb{C}$onversation should touch everything but should
concentrate itself on nothing.

The Critic as Artist

Portrait of Oscar Wilde
AUBREY BEARDSLEY 1872–1898

Private View 1881
WILLIAM POWELL FRITH 1819–1909

*T*HERE is a good deal to be said for blushing,
  if one can do it at the proper moment.

A Woman of No Importance

*T*HEY do not sin at all;
  Who sin for love.

The Duchess of Padua

*T*IRED of being on the heights
  I deliberately went to the depths
  in the search for new sensations.

De Profundis

Portrait of Oscar Wilde 1895
HENRI DE TOULOUSE-LAUTREC 1864–1901

*E*VERY GREAT man nowadays has
his disciples and it is always Judas
who writes the biography.

The Critic as Artist

I SOMETIMES think that God, in creating man,
somewhat over-estimated His ability.

In Conversation

*W*HENEVER a man does a
thoroughly stupid thing,
it is always from the noblest of motives.

The Picture of Dorian Gray

A THING is not necessarily true because a man dies for it.

The Portrait of Mr. W. H.

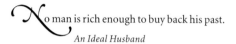

No man is rich enough to buy back his past.

An Ideal Husband

There are many things
that we would throw away,
if we were not afraid that
others might pick them up.

The Picture of Dorian Gray

All women have to fight with death to keep their children.
Death, being childless, wants our children from us.

A Woman of No Importance

The bond of all companionship,
whether in marriage or in friendship,
is conversation.

De Profundis

Caricature of Oscar Wilde

Drawing of Oscar Wilde
MAX BEERBOHM 1872–1956

Fashion is what one wears oneself.
What is unfashionable is what other people wear.

An Ideal Husband

I SHALL never make a new friend in my life,
though perhaps a few after I die.

In Conversation

One could never pay too high a price for any sensation.

The Picture of Dorian Gray

I LIKE talking to a brick wall –
it's the only thing in the world that
never contradicts me!

Lady Windermere's Fan

*A*MBITION is the last refuge of the failure.
Phrases and Philosophies for the use of the Young

*P*EOPLE ARE very fond of giving
away what they need most themselves.
It is what I call the depth of generosity.

The Picture of Dorian Gray

I always pass on good advice.
It is the only thing to do with it.
It is never any use to oneself.

An Ideal Husband

*P*LEASURE IS Nature's test, her sign of approval.
When man is happy,
he is in harmony with himself and his environment.

The Soul of Man under Socialism

An Entertaining Evening 1895
THEOPHILE-ALEXANDRE STEINLEN 1859–1923

Water Snakes I 1904–1907
GUSTAV KLIMT 1862–1918

A cynic is a man who knows the price of everything and the value of nothing.

Lady Windermere's Fan

*G*OOD TASTE is the excuse I've always given for leading such a bad life.

The Importance of Being Earnest

*N*othing ages like happiness.

The Importance of Being Earnest

*T*HE ONE advantage of playing with fire is that one never gets even singed. It is the people who don't know how to play with it who get burned up.

A Woman of No Importance

*T*HE ONLY way to get rid
of a temptation is to yield to it.

The Picture of Dorian Gray

*N*o great artist ever
sees things as they really are.
If he did he would cease to
be an artist.

The Decay of Living

*I*t is only an auctioneer who can equally and
impartially admire all schools of Art.

The Critic as Artist

Sybil in 'The Picture of Dorian Gray' 1891

At the Moulin Rouge 1892
HENRI DE TOULOUSE-LAUTREC 1864–1901

THE MAN who sees
both sides of a question
is a man who sees absolutely
nothing at all.

The Critic as Artist

*I*t is quite remarkable
how one good action always breeds another.

The Devoted Friend

THE CLEVER people never listen,
and the stupid people never talk.

A Woman of No Importance

When one is in love,
one always begins by deceiving oneself;
and one always ends by deceiving others.
That is what the world calls a romance.

The Picture of Dorian Gray

Man is least himself when he talks in his own person. Give him a mask, and he will tell you the truth.

The Critic as Artist

Illustration for Salomé 1891
AUBREY BEARDSLEY
1872–1898

I never put off till tomorrow
what I can possibly do –
the day after.

In Conversation

I n the soul of one who is ignorant
there is always room for a great idea.

De Profundis

I like to do all the talking myself.
It saves time and prevents arguments.

The Remarkable Rocket

Caricature of Oscar Wilde
VANITY FAIR 1884

To get back my youth I would do anything in the world,
except take exercise,
get up early,
or be respectable.

The Picture of Dorian Gray

A truth
ceases to be true
when more than one person believes in it.

*Phrases and Philosophies
for the use of the Young*

Memory is the diary that we all carry about with us.

The Importance of Being Earnest

*P*OETS ARE not so scrupulous as you are.
      They know how useful passion is for publication.
Nowadays a broken heart will run to many editions.

The Picture of Dorian Gray

*T*HE SOUL is born old but grows young.
    That is the comedy of life.
    And the body is born young and grows old.
    That is life's tragedy.

A Woman of No Importance

*P*EOPLE WHO who count their chickens
      before they are hatched act very wisely,
because chickens run about so absurdly that it is impossible
to count them accurately.

Letter from Paris, May 1900

Oscar Wilde lecturing in America

MAX BEERBOHM 1872–1956

Oscar Wilde – aesthete – 1882

*I*t is the confession, not the priest, that gives us absolution.

The Picture of Dorian Gray

*K*naves nowaday look so honest that
honest folk are forced to look like knaves
so as to be different.

The Duchess of Padua

*E*xperience is the name
everyone gives to their mistakes.

Lady Windermere's Fan

*M*issionaries, my dear!
Don't you realise that missionaries are the divinely
provided food for destitute and underfed cannibals?
Whenever they are on the brink of starvation,
Heaven in its infinite mercy sends them a nice plump missionary.

In Conversation

What is the good of friendship
if one cannot say exactly what one means?
Anybody can say charming things and try to please and flatter,
but a true friend always says unpleasant things,
and does not mind giving pain.

The Devoted Friend

I LIKE PERSONS better than principles and
I LIKE PERSONS with no principles better than anything in the world.

The Picture of Dorian Gray

THE OLD believe everything;
the middle-aged suspect everything;
the young know everything.

*Phrases and Philosophies
for the use of the Young*

Portrait of Oscar Wilde 1885

An acquaintance that begins with
a compliment is sure to develop into a real friendship.
It starts in the right manner.

An Ideal Husband

Anybody can make history.
Only a great man can write it.

The Critic as Artist

My own business always bores me to death.
I prefer other people's.

Lady Windermere's Fan

CHILDREN BEGIN by loving their parents.
After a time they judge them.
Rarely, if ever, do they forgive them.

A Woman of No Importance

Cartoon entitled
'Oscar, when he is ready to go'

Young men want to be faithful, and are not;
old men want to be faithless, and cannot.

The Picture of Dorian Gray

What a pity that in life we only get our
lessons when they are of no use to us!

Lady Windermere's Fan

Give me the luxuries,
and anyone can have the necessaries.

In Conversation

Portrait of Oscar Wilde c. 1894

Portrait of Oscar Wilde

A bishop keeps on saying at the age of eighty what he was told to say when he was a boy of eighteen, and as a natural consequence he always looks absolutely delightful.

The Picture of Dorian Gray

EVEN MEN of the noblest possible moral character are extremely susceptible to the influence of the physical charms of others.

The Importance of Being Earnest

One should always play fairly – when one has the winning cards.

An Ideal Husband

It is a terrible thing for a man to find out suddenly that all his life he has been speaking nothing but the truth.

The Importance of Being Earnest

*K*eep love in your heart.
A life without it is like a sunless garden
when the flowers are dead.
The consciousness of loving and being
loved brings a warmth and richness to
life that nothing else can bring.

In Conversation

*W*e teach people how to remember,
we never teach them how to grow.

The Critic as Artist

IDEALS are dangerous things.
REALITIES are better.

Lady Windermere's Fan

The Circus 1891
GEORGES SEURAT 1859–1891

The Dancer 1895
HENRI DE TOULOUSE-LAUTREC 1864–1901

I n her dealings with man Destiny never closes her accounts.

The Picture of Dorian Gray

A s soon as people are old enough to know better, they don't know anything at all.

Lady Windermere's Fan

M AN CAN believe the impossible, but man can never believe the improbable.

The Decay of Lying

W hat people call insincerity is simply a method by which we can multiply our personalities.

The Critic as Artist

Divan Japonais
HENRI DE TOULOUSE-LAUTREC 1864–1901

To love oneself is the beginning of a lifelong romance.

An Ideal Husband

Whenever people agree with me,
I always feel I must be wrong.

Lady Windermere's Fan

CONSCIENCE and cowardice are really the same things . . .
CONSCIENCE is the trade name of the firm.
                                        That is all.

The Picture of Dorian Gray

ALSO IN THIS SERIES
William Shakespeare Quotations
Winston Churchill Quotations

ALSO AVAILABLE
Little Book of Humorous Quotations
Little Book of Naughty Quotations
Little Book of Wisdom
Little Book of Wit

First published in Great Britain in 1998 by
Jarrold Publishing Ltd
Whitefriars, Norwich NR3 1TR

Developed and produced by
The Bridgewater Book Company

Researched and selected by David Notley
Picture research by Vanessa Fletcher
Printed and bound in Belgium

Copyright © 1998 Jarrold Publishing Ltd

ISBN 0–7117–1045–7

ACKNOWLEDGEMENTS
Jarrold Publishing Ltd would like to thank all those who
kindly gave permission to reproduce the words and visual material
in this book: copyright holders have been identified where possible
and we apologise for any inadvertent omissions.

We would particularly like to thank the following for the use of pictures:
Archiv für Kunst und Geschichte, London; The Bridgeman Art Library, Corbis,
Fine Art Photographic Library.

FRONT AND BACK COVER
Oscar Wilde c. 1894 (Archiv für Kunst und Geschichte, London)

FRONTISPIECE
Oscar Wilde during his lecture tour through America 1882 (Corbis)

ENDPAPERS
Oscar Wilde relaxing during his tour of America 1882 (Corbis)